RETIRE!
DEAL WITH IT!

BY
Jan King

ILLUSTRATED BY
Don Smith

CCC PUBLICATIONS

MW01609644

Published by

CCC Publications
1111 Rancho Conejo Blvd.
Suites 411 & 412
Newbury Park, CA 91320

Manufactured in the United States of America

Cover © 1997 CCC Publications

Interior illustrations © 1994 CCC Publications

Cover art by Charles Goll

Interior art by Don Smith

Interior layout & production by Oasis Graphics

ISBN: 1-57644-057-5

If your local U.S. bookstore is out of stock, copies of this book may be obtained by mailing check or money order for $4.99 per book (plus $2.50 to cover postage and handling) to: CCC Publications, 1111 Rancho Conejo Blvd., Suites 411 & 412, Newbury Park, CA 91320

First Printing - 1/97

INTRODUCTION

You have paid off the mortgage, raised your kids, and painted your house for the last time. Now your life can become ONE BIG GAME of the Retirement Olympics!

So take the challenge. The following pages are filled with the inevitable "games" every Senior participates in sooner or later. Keep a running score to see just how much of a "pro" you are already and what you have to do to reach the ultimate goal of Senior Olympiad!

THE I-95 INDY: Gentlemen Start Your Engines

Every fall, a caravan of cars, RV's, and motor homes driven by crazed retirees hit the highway like clockwork. They are all heading to Florida at 85m.p.h., trying to avoid the speed traps and still make it in 24 hours or less. The whole turnpike becomes an Indy 500 of Speeding Seniors, recklessly weaving in and out of traffic, attempting to make it down to their condos faster than the speed of light.

And even though they don't have a thing booked on their social calendars for six months, they're still willing to risk losing vital body parts to gain an extra day on the patio, sloshing down a bucket of margaritas.

IF THIS DESCRIBES YOU, SCORE 1 POINT: ☐

THE EQUIPMENT: Positive I.D. Of The Retiree's Car

- Golf caps and sun visors piled so high in the rear window as to totally obstruct vision.

- Hanging clothes racks loaded with 100% polyester pastel pants, loud plaid jackets, and elastic waisted slacks.

- Those dumpy-looking storage bins on the car roof racks stuffed with beach towels and other assorted clothes flapping out of the sides.

- Fuzz busters prominently displayed on the dashboard.

- Watchman TV plugged into the cigarette lighter so as not to miss a single episode of "Days Of Our Lives."

- Well-stocked bar and Coleman ice chests packed with snacks and sandwiches. The driver stops for no one. Bathroom pits stops are granted only once in every eight hour period.

- Full scale assortment of religious statuary across the dashboard. Wives clutch their rosary beads with eyes shut tight and lips moving rapidly in silent prayer for safe arrival.

SCORE 1 POINT FOR EACH THAT APPLIES TO YOUR CAR:

FUN SENIOR CAR GAMES: How Time Flies When You're Having A Fight!

Here are some popular senior time-passers while heading to the old retirement condo:

- Bicker with the spouse for a 150 mile stretch about whose fault it was that you exited off the wrong ramp and got lost for two hours.

- Count Stuckey and Burma Shave signs along the highway until you begin to hallucinate.

- Look for familiar faces of fellow retirees you pass each year on the road to Florida—then discuss how much paler and sicker they look than last year.

- Sing along with Willie for the 1559th rendition of "On The Road Again."

- Bicker about things that happened 20 years ago you're still steamed about.

SCORE 1 POINT FOR EACH GAME YOU'VE PLAYED: ☐

THE TRAVEL ITINERARY GAME (Part I): I Brake For No One

Like clockwork, the retirees follow the same roadie behaviors year after year:

- Drives at 85 m.p.h. from 4 A.M. 'til 4 P.M. with left blinker going continuously.

- Pulls into Holiday Inn at 4 P.M. to take advantage of 50 cent margaritas and three-day-old tacos featured at "Happy Hour."

- Bargain Senior Citizen room rate of $29.95 booked one year in advance, includes cot and complimentary breakfast of half-perked coffee and donuts with filling of unknown origin.

- Room location chosen for direct access to the ice-maker. Booze and mixers are brought in from the car by whichever spouse is best able to walk after the extended cocktail hour.

SCORE 1 POINT FOR EACH GAME YOU'VE PLAYED: ☐

THE TRAVEL ITINERARY GAME (Part II): If You Snooze You Loose

- One scheduled pit-stop in North Carolina to load the trunk with cartons of cigarettes purchased at cheap bootleg prices from a burly saleswoman sporting a tatoo of her bearded Mother on her biceps.

- Avoids any possibility of falling asleep at the wheel by consuming one small Stuckey's pecan pie. This keeps him wired from the 10 hour sugar jolt it packs.

- Keeps his blood circulating and his muscles relaxed by using one of those fatigue-fighting wooden ball seat covers endorsed by every non-English-speaking cab driver in N.Y. City.

- Keeps a couple of snorts on tap to numb the pain in case one of the seat cover's massaging balls breaks loose and ends up in an excruciatingly inextricable location.

SCORE 1 POINT FOR EACH GAME YOU'VE PLAYED:

THE SPORT OF BUYING YOUR DOUBLE-WIDE MOBILE HOME:
Beware Of Men In Plaid

Trailer parks have become the answer to the retiree's quest for affordable housing. And you won't ever have to look for a salesperson—they'll find you!! They'll hunt you down in every AARP meeting hall, supermarket, or discount department store in America.

Armed with hundreds of color brochures which make the dirt lot the mobile is situated on look like the Garden of Eden, it's hard to say no to this guy. One word of caution: don't ever refer to a mobile home as a "Trailer," because he'll drop the smarmy smile and cold-cock you right on the spot. This is a term that went out of style the same year the janitors started calling themselves "maintenance engineers."

SCORE 1 POINT IF YOU'VE PLAYED THIS GAME: ☐

YESSIREE, BOB! I HAVE JUST THE NUMBER FOR YOU! IT'S A SLIGHTLY USED DOUBLE WIDE, **AL**MOST FIRE RESISTANT, **S**EMI-TORNADO-PROOF AND OWNED FOR ONLY ONE HOUR AND 45 MINUTES BY A LITTLE OLD LADY WHO DIED OF CLAUSTRAPHOBIA. NOW LET ME TELL YOU WHAT I CAN DO. FOR NOTHING DOWN, DID YOU HEAR ME, GRAMPS? I SAID **NOTHING DOWN**... AND NO PAYMENT UNTIL...

MOBILE MADNESS: Getting Revenge On The Relatives

Here's some "awesome" features of the mobile home that will make your new life one big stress-free game:

• Park 'em in the driveway of your kid's house for at least a week. You can avoid baby sitting their rude kids as well as keeping a safe distance from their constant bickering.

• If it gets to be too much, just don your Willy Nelson Stars N' Stripes Bandannas, put the pedal to the metal, and you're outta there!

• Scrawl a note on their driveway—"Thanks for everything—we'll call YOU... collect. Then dump the toilet reservoir and pull out of there like a bat out of hell.

YES!!! Total Freedom.

SCORE 1 POINT FOR EACH MOVE YOU'VE SUCCESSFULLY PULLED OFF: ☐

MOBILE PARKS: Playing Against The Odds

These are the types of daily activities enjoyed by all Seniors who live in their beloved Florida trailer parks.

Over your morning coffee and daily newspaper, you go straight to the obit page to see who's kicked the bucket. The stats add up to approximately 10 goners a month. Typically, this is the breakdown:

• 3 coronaries

• 2 old age

• 1 boredom from checkers

• 3 alligator mishaps

• 1 drowning (accidentally driving the car into the canal)

Then in the afternoon, the mobile "bookie" takes $2.00 bets on your guess at the number of residents who will break their hip that week.

SCORE 1 POINT FOR BEATING THE ODDS IN EACH SITUATION:

THE MOBILE DECORATION COMPETITION: Lighten Up

Another community activity of mobile owners is to decorate the yard with statuary year 'round. It's the hottest competition in the Senior Mobile Olympics—seeing who can most creatively fill their lots with plastic flamingos, ceramic turtles, and wooden ducks with spinning wings. Many of these mobile lots have actually been declared as National Wildlife Preserves For Decoys.

But the fastest and most furious competition is at Christmas when the folks totally O.D. on decorating. Zillions of multi-colored lights are strung around entire nativity scenes, flamingo necks, and decorated palm trees, until the whole area is so illuminated it looks like a landing strip for DC 10's.

SCORE 1 POINT FOR PARTICIPATING IN THE DECORATING COMPETITION: ☐

SENIOR SPORTS: Tennis

All Seniors equipment of choice are those huge over-sized racquets that look like hula-hoops with handles. This way, they can field the ball within a 50 foot radius without ever having to move their feet.

They just stand there and watch the ball coming towards them; hold out their arm with the giant racquet head and let the ball deflect off of it. But never underestimate the strategy used by these over-the-hillers. They are really experts at lobbing. You can rush the net and hit a 95 mph power shot at them and they'll lob it back over your head forcing you to run your tush all over the court on every shot. Naturally, you'll miss the return 99% of the time. This leaves you looking like a total dork, as they whip your butt 6-0 6-0 in front of their cheering cronies.

GIVE YOURSELF 1 POINT FOR USING THESE TENNIS TACTICS: ☐

GOLFING: No Sudden Death Here

After having read about hundreds of other Seniors dropping dead on the 18th hole, the over-the-hiller approaches golf in a more cautious fashion. They do not want to push their heart muscles too far by walking 3 or 4 holes. So they ride in their own customized golf carts, with a blood pressure cuff and equipped with small pharmacies. Smartly, they have their cardiologists doubling as their caddies.

Rather than chance a sudden squall with wind, rain and hazardous lightning, the Senior is always prepared by wearing his full-length clear plastic raincoat. So when you see a group ahead on the greens who look like walking condoms, you'll know what age category they fall into.

SCORE 1 POINT IF YOU HAVE THE MEDICAL GOLF CART AND 2 POINTS FOR LOOKING LIKE A CONDOM ON THE COURSE:

THE SPORT DOMINATED BY SENIORS: Bingo

This game is mandatory for any self-respecting over-the-hiller past fifty. These guys and gals have mastered playing 10 to 15 cards simultaneously and clean up those jackpots before the younger player can find G-53 on his bingo card. Yes, this group is really into finding their G spots!

Their concentration level is so intense, if they channeled their energy, they could levitate the jockey shorts off Doug Henning.

SCORE 1 POINT FOR EACH DAY OF THE WEEK YOU PLAY BINGO: ☐

SENIOR BIRTHDAYS:
You'll Need A Garden Hose To Put Out Those Candles

Many Seniors turn into the world's biggest party poopers when they have to celebrate their own birthdays. They all say the same thing to mark the occasion:

"Well, I better enjoy this one because it's probably going to be my last."

Lighten up, folks. It's a bummer for all the other Seniors dressed in party hats and ready to rock n' roll. If you keep it up, it WILL be your last birthday—because these hip party-goers are going to head someplace else where they won't have to swallow a handful of mood elevators along with your birthday cake.

GIVE YOURSELF 1 POINT FOR EVERY BIRTHDAY PAST 65 THAT YOU HAVE MADE THIS STATEMENT: ☐

TOTAL TOGETHERNESS: Thermostat Wars

The newly retired husband will go on a purge to save money. The first thing he will do is fire your cleaning lady and appoint himself as your new "Cleaning Gestapo." Here's what you're in for:

- While you're dusting, he's right on your tail wearing white gloves, fingering every spot you missed.

- He'll stack the dishwasher with everything from dirty dishes to dirty underwear. And then he'll only let you run it during the "energy efficient" hours of 2-4 A.M.

- He'll do the laundry, mixing whites with colors in boiling hot water. The dryer is always set on HIGH, and he'll turn it off only when he smells something BURNING.

- He'll commandeer the thermostat and keep it on a "comfortable" 50 degrees all winter. In the summer, he'll only turn on the air conditioning after the pets shrivel from dehydration or algae grows on the wallpaper from the heat and humidity.

BE HONEST. SCORE 1 POINT FOR EACH OF THESE YOU DO: ☐

RULES FOR VISITING YOUR RETIRED PARENTS: Valium Vacations

Warning: Here's some visiting situations that will drive your retired parents straight to their Prozac and Valium stash in the cookie jar:

- If they invite you to dinner at 6 P.M., realize that they will be dressed and ready by 4 P.M. They'll sit and watch every tick of the clock until you arrive. At 6:05 they're pacing, at 6:10 they're groaning, and by 6:15 smoke is pouring out of their ears. Anything from 6:15 on—you better be armed when you go through their door.

- Be prepared for three-day lectures on how you aren't disciplining your kids. They'll suggest you put them all in military school.

- Don't bring your teenagers into your parent's home if they're wearing:

    a. pierced ear, nose, or nipple jewelry

    b. neon spiky hair or shaved skinheads

    c. T-shirts picturing heavy metal bands eating live   rodents

    d. leather studded bustiers, fishnet stockings, or   neoprene bras

    e. "I Practice Safe Sex" buttons.

SENIORS SCORE 1 POINT FOR EACH BEHAVIOR YOU EXHIBIT: ☐

MORE RULES FOR VISITING YOUR PARENTS: Stayin' Alive

- If you're a divorced daughter, NEVER ask if you and the new boyfriend can sleep together under their roof. You'll always be Daddy's little girl, 40 years old or not. Be prepared for a three-hour sermon on immorality, which he took word for word, straight from the lips of his idol—Jimmy Swaggart.

- Never interfere with the folks' TV programs. They'll never give up "The Price Is Right" or "Wheel Of Fortune" so you can watch CNN. Any tampering with the TV lineup could disorient them to the point where they're eating bran flakes with the 11 P.M. news.

- To avoid giving your Dad "The Big One" when he insists on driving you around town—DON'T:

    a. scream while he's pulling a U-ey across 4 lanes of   traffic

    b. maintain a death grip on the dashboard

    c. cover your eyes while he's tailgating at 85 m.p.h.

SCORE 1 POINT FOR EACH THING YOUR KIDS DID THAT IRRITATED TO YOU: ☐

THE SENIOR MEDICAL CHALLENGE: Go With The Flow

Here's the most popular body parts and body functions that over-the-hillers obsess about:

- CONSTIPATION—makes Seniors load up on so much fiber and bran, they need to install a seat belt on their johns.

- BREAKING A HIP— will eliminate all activities from golf to sex. You'll need a new marital aid (like a rope and pulley rented from the Flying Wallendas) in order to have sex in a hip cast.

- CHOLESTEROL—something Seniors count more frequently than their money.

- DENTURES— Seniors never go anywhere without packing a tube of Poly-Grip. And to insure a tight fit, many retirees dispense it with a caulking gun.

- HIATAL AND OTHER HERNIAS—at this age you can get a hernia from just about any activity including sucking on a straw or picking lint out of your belly button.

SCORE 1 POINT FOR EACH MEDICAL CHALLENGE YOU'VE EXPERIENCED: ☐

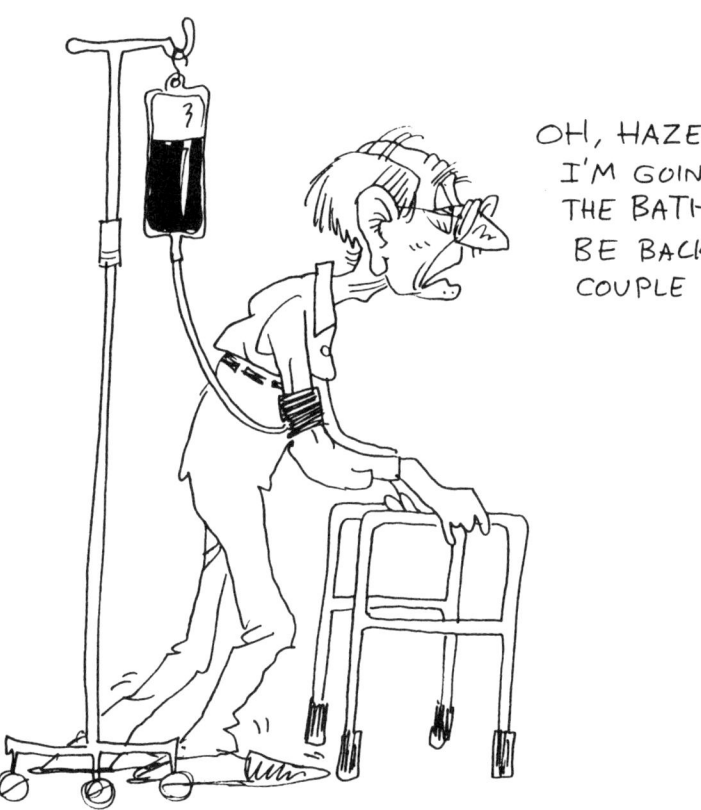

THE ALL-PRO PROSTATE COMPETITION: Plugging The Leaks

Senior men have a male bonding thing going on with their urologists. The minute they step into his office, on reflex they drop their pants, bend over, and cough. Does the phrase "enlarged prostate" ring a bell? Rather than have that big ole catheter inserted into their private part, most men would just as soon let it fall off and roll down the street.

LET'S SCORE 1 POINT FOR THE OL' PROSTATE: ☐

[TO BE FAIR, <u>WOMEN</u> SCORE ONE POINT IF YOUR HUSBAND HAS A BLOWN-UP PROSTATE]: ☐

WE HAD A PARTY FOR
WILLARD LAST NIGHT.
REAL EMOTIONAL OCCASION!
THERE WASN'T A DRY SEAT
IN THE HOUSE.

PLAYING BY THE RULES: The Good Old G.P. Game

This Family Doctor has been treating you for 40 years, even though he should have hung up his stethoscope in the late 50's. But he's hell-bent on practicing until it kills him—or you. He's been dispensing the same advice for 40 years:

"You're just getting old. Go home and take a hot bath."

Nowadays, the old geeze is so hard of hearing, you'll have to spell out your symptoms using semaphore. But he makes you feel good and secure, like being with your Grandpa again. So no matter how doddering he gets, you're sticking with him like Poly-Grip.

SCORE 1 POINT IF YOUR G.P. IS OVER 80: ☐

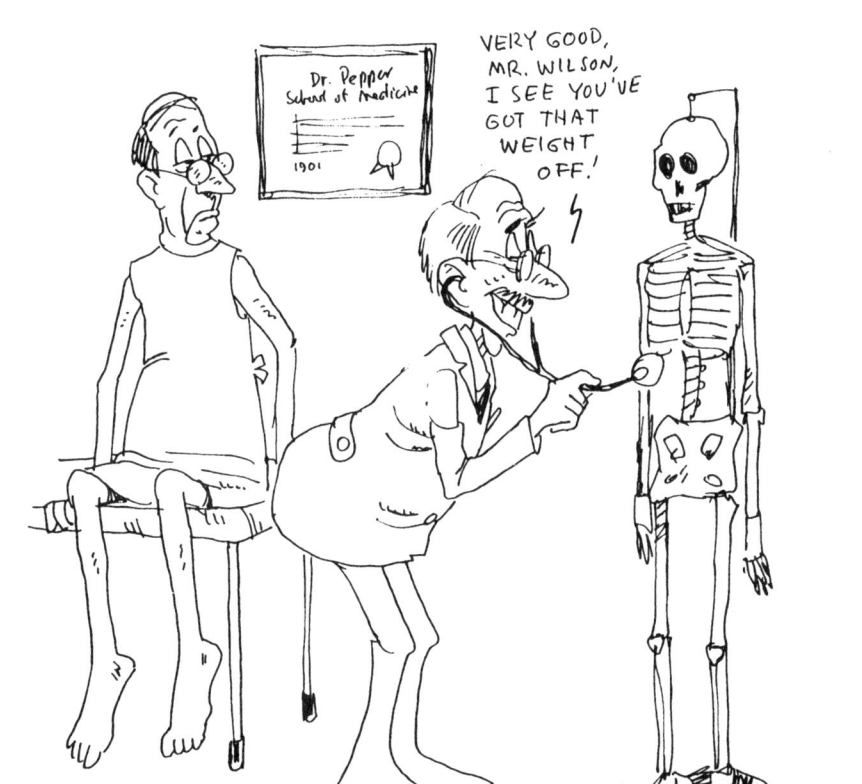

THE OVER-THE-HILL SEX CHALLENGE: Anything Is Possible

While younger America is obsessing over the following topics, over-the-hillers never give them a second thought:

- **PREMATURE EJACULATION**—they're just happy to have one—premature or not

- **SPERM COUNT**—just like their birthdays, they stopped counting years ago

- **SAFE SEX**—to over-the-hillers, it means extra padding on the headboard

- **SIMULTANEOUS ORGASMS**—seniors are used to their bodies taking more time to respond to everything— so anything within a couple of days is acceptable.

- **STAYING POWER**—is for young studs. The only thing over-the hillers are interested in is staying **AWAKE**.

- **CONDOMS**—a thing of the past. The only slim, foil-wrapped package he'll be opening in the dark is his Alka-Seltzer.

SCORE 1 POINT FOR EACH SEXUAL CHALLENGE YOU'VE CONQUERED: ☐

IT'S YOUR TURN TO MOVE.

NO IT'S YOURS.

I MOVED LAST
TIME.

ZZZZZZZ

THE ODDS FOR SENIOR SEX: All Bets Are Off

- **MEN:** before beginning any sexual activity, for your own safety, remove that rupture truss.

- **LADIES:** to prevent serious injury to any male body part, before beginning foreplay, secure your dentures with Poly-Grip.

- **LADIES:** be seductive. Wear a black lace garter belt—but be sure to remove your support hose first.

- Practice safe sex—don't ever try jump-starting marital aids with your pacemaker batteries.

- Don't let premature ejaculation dampen your sex lives. Try starting a couple of hours BEFORE him.

SCORE 1 POINT FOR EACH SAFE SEX TECHNIQUE YOU REGULARLY USE: ☐

ODDS ON SEX: Play It Where It Lays OR Lay It Where It Plays

- To heighten arousal in your partner—do some heavy breathing directly into each others bel-Tones.

- Experiment with new positions—hit those "raise," "lower," and "massage" buttons on your motorized bed.

- MEN: you must remove the cigar before attempting to French kiss the missus.

- LADIES: talk dirty during sex—it's highly stimulating. But keep it under 5 minutes and DON'T drop the receiver on him during orgasm.

SCORE 1 POINT FOR EACH ACTIVITY YOU'VE DONE DURING SEX: ☐

YOU YOUNG PEOPLE
GET TURNED ON
BY HEAVY BREATHING!
HEY! I'M GRATEFUL
IF MY PARTNER IS
BREATHING AT ALL!

THE MATURE MARRIAGE GAME: Joined At The Hip

Here's some good reasons why getting married late in life will make for a longer marriage:

• Too old to care if he puts the cap back on the Poly-Grip.

• Enjoy "gourmet" foods together—like apricot Jello at every meal.

• Amuse themselves with spur of the moment sports—like Saturday afternoon walker races.

• Look forward to getting regularly "ripped" together at 3 o' clock cocktail hour on "Maalox Gin Fizzes."

• Low risk of having unwanted love child.

• Have a ball together playing pranks with "First Alert" buttons.

SCORE 1 POINT FOR EACH MARRIAGE GAME YOU PLAY: ⬜

RACING TO THOSE EARLY BIRD SPECIALS:
Happy Hour At The Salad Bar

Retirees show up between 4-6 P.M. to beat the crowds and take advantage of the great bargain menus. The salad bar offers a huge variety of foods with absolutely no nutritional value. You can stuff your faces with:

- plasticized bacon bits
- waxed green beans (with Pledge)
- boulder-sized croutons
- those popular colon busters: Garbanzo Beans
- alfalfa sprouts organically grown in bat guano
- Cheez-Whiz macaroni salads
- pickled beets containing enough red dye #5 to keep your urine pink for three days
- canned lead-lite fruits

SCORE 1 POINT FOR EACH GOURMET SERVING YOU'VE SAMPLED: ☐

TAKING COUPON CHALLENGE: Two-Fer Tea

Seniors love to comb the newspapers and local penny-saver magazines in search of those two-for-one coupons. However, always read the **FINE PRINT**. Sometimes you'll find more restrictions than a parolee faces upon release from jail. If you read the coupon carefully, you can avoid a major duke-out in the parking lot with a manager who refused to honor it, because the two-fer:

• is for one regular meal—over $59.95

• is for one adult and a companion with no teeth

• coupon expires after 2 P.M. on the same day it appears in the paper

• is only good for the table next to the restrooms

SCORE 1 POINT FOR EACH MAJOR FIGHT OVER ANY OF THESE COUPON RESTRICTIONS:

LESSEE NOW, BY MY CALCULATION THESE 534 COUPONS ADD UP TO 72 CENTS OFF - BUT MEBBE I'D BETTER COUNT 'EM AGAIN.
YOU CAN'T BE TOO CAREFUL, I ALWAYS SAY

MOONLIGHT MADNESS OLYMPICS: Up For Grabs

These can be more physically challenging than an appearance on the "American Gladiators." Many seniors go into training to bulk up for this crowd-fighting event where lightening quick reflexes are crucial for grabbing merchandise from sale tables.

Arrive at the door hours early, so as to be one of the first 100 people to receive a free LED watch (it stops working before you get back to the parking lot). Your training will provide the keen eye and the quick hand you'll need to snatch the last pair of 100% poly-socks from the fat pig who is shoving you out of her way.

SCORE 3 POINTS IF YOU HAVE SUCCESSFULLY TRAINED FOR THE MOONLIGHT OLYMPICS: ☐

SENIOR DRIVERS PLATES: A Crash Course

Suggested personalized plates for "hip" drivers:

I BRK 4 NO 1   2 OLD 2 C

20/20 VIZON   UZ NO SIGNL

35 MPH MAX   SGL L GO R

SLO 2 REACT   FREQ STPS

NO EEG WAVS   NRVZ SHOT

SCORE 1 POINT IF YOU HAVE A PERSONALIZED SENIOR LICENSE PLATE: ☐

"ON BOARD" WARNINGS: Read The Fine Print Carefully

- Pacemaker On Board
- Frequent Pit Stops
- Caution: Driver Withdrawing From Prozac
- Easily Rattled
- Heavily Insured For Collision
- Driver Takes Frequent Naps
- Cheated On Eye Test
- Junker Car: Nothing To Lose
- Full Load: Driver Wearing Depends

SCORE 1 POINT FOR EACH SIGN YOU DISPLAY: ☐

THE MEDICATION MANIA CHALLENGE: Generically Yours

Over-the-hillers are becoming more knowledgeable than pharmacists. They can tell you which generic brands work best, which cold and flu remedy is most effective, and everything you never wanted to know about Fleets Enemas. They buy the following in bulk quantities:

HAILEY'S MO—used as a chaser following a stiff prune juice cocktail. Make sure you time it properly. You don't want it suddenly "kicking in" during the middle of an all-day bus tour.

AFRIN— beware: you can get so hooked on sniffing this stuff up your nose three times a day that, without it, your nasal mucus turns to concrete.

FLEX-All—if Joe Namath recommends it, every guy in America over 40 is going to buy it. Of course, they'll never suffer the kind of muscle soreness Joe had after football. But there's always hope they'll be lucky enough to have the same muscle soreness he had after his BEDROOM games.

SCORE 1 POINT FOR EACH MEDICATION YOU'VE ABUSED:

WHERE'S THE FLEX-ALL? I'VE BEEN WATCHIN' FOOTBALL SO LONG I CAN HARDLY MOVE!

SENIOR PRODUCTS ROULETTE: May The Odds Be With You

DR. SCHOLL'S FOOT PRODUCTS— where would we be without good old Dr. Scholl? At home with our sore dogs soaking in a bucket of Epsom Salts, that's where. The doc manufactures everything from bunion and corn plasters to air-foam insoles. These have made him so popular, his name ranks up there with Ghandi's. In fact, many seniors list Scholl on their medical forms as their family doctor.

DEPENDS— let's face it—after 40, leaky bladders happen. But we certainly don't need June Allyson bustling around in her taffeta dress, pointing out all the people in the room who have just wet their pants. But if your friends need to throw you a life preserver every time you`laugh, you definitely need this product.

SCORE 1 POINT FOR EACH SENIOR PRODUCT YOU'VE BOUGHT: ☐

A Lifetime of Doctors

DR. SEUSS

DR. DENTON

DR. SPOCK

DR. HOOK

DR. SCHOLL

SCORE CARD

0-50   **AMATEUR** (Turn In Your AARP Card You Fraud!)

51-89   **JUNIOR LIGHTWEIGHT** (You're Ready To Start Wearing Black Socks And Sandals)

90-120   **ADVANCED INTERMEDIATE** (Eligible To Carry Leather Coupon Case)

121+   **ALL-PRO SENIOR CITIZEN** (You Can Make A U-Turn Anywhere You Please On The Highway)